Beyond Reproach

Rising Above Gossip in the Workplace

By Shawntel D. Carey

SDC Compass Publishling

Beyond Reproach
Rising Above Gossip in the Workplace

Written by Shawntel D. Carey, MPA

Published by SDC Compass Publishing LLC
Lawrenceville, Georgia

Interior and layout design by Shawntel D. Carey
Illustrations source is Canva Pro licensed use

Printed in the United States of America

eBook ISBN: 979-8-9939033-2-3
Print ISBN: 979-8-9939033-4-7

DEDICATION

Dedicated to

Prof. Trudy Dunson- Wilson

Program Director, Business Management, Gwinnett Technical College,

who instructed me, mentored me, and helped shape the professional

I am today. Your influence lives in this work.

The Author

SHAWNTEL D. CAREY, MPA

Shawntel is an entrepreneur, author, publisher, and public servant with a strong background across the public, private, and nonprofit sectors. She brings a practical, people-centered approach to leadership and workplace culture, shaped by her experience bridging business, policy, and community in a way that creates meaningful impact.

Shawntel understands how gossip, miscommunication, and workplace drama can derail careers and damage morale. The principle of avoiding gossip has guided her across every role, consistently choosing integrity over disruption.

She is the author of Words to Live By: Quotes by Shawntel D. Carey and Civic Adventures: How Individuals, Families, and Communities Learn Together. Her work reflects her tried and true experience, personal growth, and a commitment to helping people lead with clarity, confidence, and character.

TABLE OF CONTENTS

SHAWNTEL D. CAREY

Introduction

 Beyond Reproach: Rising Above Gossip in the Workplace

Introduction

"I urge you to welcome the challenge!"
-Shawntel D. Carey, 2022

These words are not just a personal statement; they are professional convictions. Gossip is often overlooked as "harmless chatter," but in the workplace, it erodes trust, stifles progress and leaves lasting stains on reputations. Having witnessed and experienced the subtle yet damaging effects of gossip, I believe it is one of the greatest hindrances to professional growth and a silent barrier to leadership. This book is written primarily for young professionals but may serve as a gentle reminder to all professionals who desire not only to excel in their careers but to live a life that is above reproach, marked by integrity and respect.

You can change your life...
if you purposefully change your thoughts.

-Shawntel D. Carey, 2019

From Words to Live By: Quotes by Shawntel D. Carey

SHAWNTEL D. CAREY

The Reflection That Inspired This Book

 Beyond Reproach: Rising Above Gossip in the Workplace

The Reflection That Inspired This Book

"I loathe gossip but particularly in a professional capacity."

There was a moment in my professional journey when I realized just how damaging gossip can be, not only to careers, but to confidence, productivity, and reputation. I have observed individuals with incredible potential get caught up in conversations that led nowhere, and I noticed that those who engaged in gossip rarely grew into leadership roles.

As a young professional myself, I was tempted to join in. I wanted to fit in. I wanted to be liked. Fortunately, my mentors encouraged me to reflect on the qualities of leadership I aspired to embody and the reputation I sought to establish through my character. They helped me understand that gossip leaves a stain on one's reputation, and once applied, it is difficult to remove.

So, I developed a simple approach. When a conversation shifted toward gossip, I would listen respectfully, and when the moment came for me to participate, I would say, "Although I find your conversation interesting, I don't gossip." Then I would gently excuse myself.

Over time, something changed. Individuals began approaching me solely to discuss substantive matters. I gained respect. And I learned that professionalism is not only about performance, but also about character.

This book was born from that understanding. While it is written with young professionals in mind, it is for anyone who desires to rise beyond gossip, protect their reputation, and lead with integrity and purpose.

Shawntel D. Carey, MPA

CHAPTER ONE

The Nature of Gossip

 Beyond Reproach: Rising Above Gossip in the Workplace

Chapter 1: The Nature of Gossip

Gossip may seem like casual conversation, but in reality, it is a corrosive force. It thrives on speculation, misrepresentation, and negativity.

In a professional setting, those that gossip, ultimately:
• Distract from productivity.
• Create divisions among teams.
• Undermines trust and credibility.

Gossip harms the one who engages in it more than the one being discussed.

Throughout my years in the professional arena, I have observed a striking pattern: those who consistently engage in gossip rarely, if ever, ascend to executive levels.

Why? Because leadership demands discretion, integrity, and the ability to foster trust, qualities that cannot coexist with gossip.

A Stain on Your Character

 Beyond Reproach: Rising Above Gossip in the Workplace

Chapter 2: A Stain on Your Character

Your reputation is the currency of your career. Every choice, especially the choice to participate in gossip. Either it adds to or subtracts from that currency. Gossiping can gradually damage a person's reputation.

If you choose to gossip, this is what that says about you:

(1) "I cannot be trusted with sensitive information."
(2) "I find value in tearing others down instead of building them up."
(3) "My focus is on drama, not solutions."

Professionals who consistently entertain gossip may find temporary inclusion; however, they often experience long-term exclusion from leadership opportunities.

CHAPTER THREE

The Professional's Choice

Chapter 3: The Professional's Choice

As a professional, I too faced the temptation of gossip.

I wanted to belong. I wanted to be liked. And often, being included meant being complicit in conversations that were neither productive nor professional.

Fortunately, I had mentors who guided me to decide early:

• How do I want to be perceived?

• What values will I hold firmly?

• How do my dreams align with my behavior?

It was clear: if I desired a career built on respect and leadership, gossip could not be a part of my journey.

A Strategy for Rising Above

Chapter 4: A Strategy for Rising Above

A Culture of Informality

Today's workplaces have become increasingly informal, blurring the lines between professional and personal behavior.

While casual environments can encourage creativity, they can also normalize destructive habits like gossip.

As professionals, we must remember informality does not excuse unprofessionalism.

Choosing not to gossip is not about being rigid but is about setting a standard of excellence that others will recognize and admire.

Strategy for Rising Above

Avoiding gossip does not mean avoiding people. It means setting boundaries with grace and courage.

This strategy is simple yet effective:

1. Listen politely: Allow others to share what they want.

2. Respond with integrity:
Say, "Although I find your conversation interesting, I don't gossip."

3. Exit gracefully;
Excuse yourself and redirect your focus to more substantive matters.

4. The result? Earned respect.

Colleagues will began approaching you with conversations of depth, value, and purpose. Instead of being excluded, you will be entrusted with meaningful dialogue.

Living Beyond Reproach

Chapter 5: Living Beyond Reproach

Choosing not to engage in gossip isn't just for the workplace, it's a commitment that shapes your entire lifestyle.

Living beyond reproach means that your name carries weight and your presence commands respect. It is the kind of character that not only advances careers but also builds legacies.

Eleanor Roosevelt stated:

"Great minds discuss ideas; Average minds discuss events; Small minds discuss people."

Choose to be among great minds.

SHAWNTEL D. CAREY

For
Young
Professionals

 Beyond Reproach: Rising Above Gossip in the Workplace

For Young Professionals

If you aspire to lead, to build, and to leave a meaningful impact, you must reject gossip and live beyond reproach.

Not just for your career, but in your life. Hold fast to your character. Stay true to your values. Build your dreams with integrity.

And when you are invited into conversations that do not align with your vision and purpose, respond with confidence: *"I don't gossip."*

This straightforward statement may serve as a fundamental principle for achieving professional excellence.

If this message resonates with you, consider passing it along to someone who might appreciate it.

It's important for every professional to remember that genuine leadership is rooted in integrity.

SDC COMPASS PUBLISHING

The
Beyond Reproach
Collection

 Beyond Reproach: Rising Above Gossip in the Workplace

SDC Compass Publishing

OFFICIAL STORE & COLLECTIONS

The Beyond Reproach Collection reflects clarity, discipline, and purpose-driven work, designed for professional minimalists.

Stay Connected

We'd love to hear from you.

Email: sdccompasspublishing@gmail.com

For updates, new releases, and merchandise:

- LinkedIn: SDC Compass Publishing LLC
- Instagram: @SDCCompassPublishing
- Facebook: SDC Compass Publishing
- https://sdccompasspublishing.etsy.com

Beyond Reproach
Rising Above Gossip in the Workplace

Don't forget to tag us: #BeyondRepoarchCollection

SDC Compass Publishing